# What if...?

How to reframe challenges into opportunities for growth

Bronwyn Frazer

# Contents

| | |
|---|---|
| About the Author | ix |
| Introduction | xi |

**CHAPTER 1** — 1
*Learning through relationships*

| | |
|---|---|
| What if: you knew every relationship (even the difficult ones) offered a gift? | 2 |
| What if: you understood that hurt people hurt others? | 4 |
| What if: you could heal a relationship by apologising? | 6 |
| What if: you understood that no one owes you anything? | 9 |
| What if: you knew that your parents did the best they could? | 11 |
| What if: you said 'no'? | 14 |
| What if: today you looked for the good in others? | 17 |
| What if: you realised that mean people help you grow? | 19 |
| What if: you detached from the drama? | 23 |
| What if: everyone looked for similarities, instead of differences? | 26 |
| What if: you spoke up? | 29 |
| What if: you knew that nothing you have or own defines you? | 32 |
| What if: you took responsibility for your own happiness? | 34 |
| What if: you understood that words hold power? | 37 |
| What if: you learnt to forgive? | 40 |
| What if: you knew that self-love is crucial for your health? | 43 |
| What if: you stopped letting the fear of rejection hold you back? | 45 |

**CHAPTER 2** — 47
*Growing through discomfort*

- What if: you knew that resilience is a life skill? — 48
- What if: you could feel better by changing your response? — 52
- What if: you trusted that your challenge has a purpose? — 56
- What if: you let go? — 59
- What if: you trusted that everything will be ok? — 62
- What if: you learnt from your regrets? — 68
- What if: you faced your fears and danced with them anyway? — 71
- What if: you loved your body instead of criticising it? — 74
- What if: you understood that anger can be a good thing? — 77
- What if: you waited instead of rushing an important decision? — 80
- What if: you realised it is good to accept help? — 83

**CHAPTER 3** — 85
*Dealing with death*

- What if: you knew love never dies? — 86
- What if: you remembered death is part of the cycle of life? — 89
- What if: by sharing your challenge, you help people heal? — 94
- What if: you knew you didn't have long to live? — 97
- What if: you knew that only love is real? — 100

**CHAPTER 4** — 103
*Creating consciously*

- What if: your life inspired others? — 104
- What if: your random act of kindness could help someone view life differently? — 107
- What if: you focused on today, instead of the future? — 109
- What if: today you chose to be positive? — 111
- What if: you knew you could create your own luck? — 113

| | |
|---|---|
| What if: your natural gifts could help others? | 115 |
| What if: your donation could help many? | 118 |
| What if: you knew sharing increases your abundance? | 121 |
| What if: I told you that you could change a person's day, just by smiling? | 123 |
| What if: you knew kindness is a superpower? | 125 |
| What if: by being generous, you inspired a better world? | 128 |
| What if: you knew your life has a purpose? | 130 |
| What if: you could help the earth heal? | 132 |
| Acknowledgments | 135 |

*What if... ? How to reframe challenges into opportunities for growth*

By Bronwyn Frazer

© 2024 Bronwyn Frazer

www.bronwynfrazer.com.au

Hembury Books

www.hemburybooks.com.au

A copy of this book has been deposited with the Australian National Library.

All rights reserved. No portion of this book may be reproduced in any form without permission from the author and publisher, except as permitted by Australian copyright law.

The author of this book does not dispense medical advice or prescribe the use of any technique as a form of treatment for physical, emotional, mental health, or medical problems without the advice of a general practitioner (GP), either directly or indirectly. The intent of the author is only to offer guidance of a general nature to help you in your quest for emotional and spiritual well-being.

If you use any of the information in this book for yourself, which is your constitutional and legal right, the author and the publisher assume no responsibility for your actions.

For Geoff (1968 – 2009) and Joe Frazer (1938 – 2020).
Thank you for watching over me.

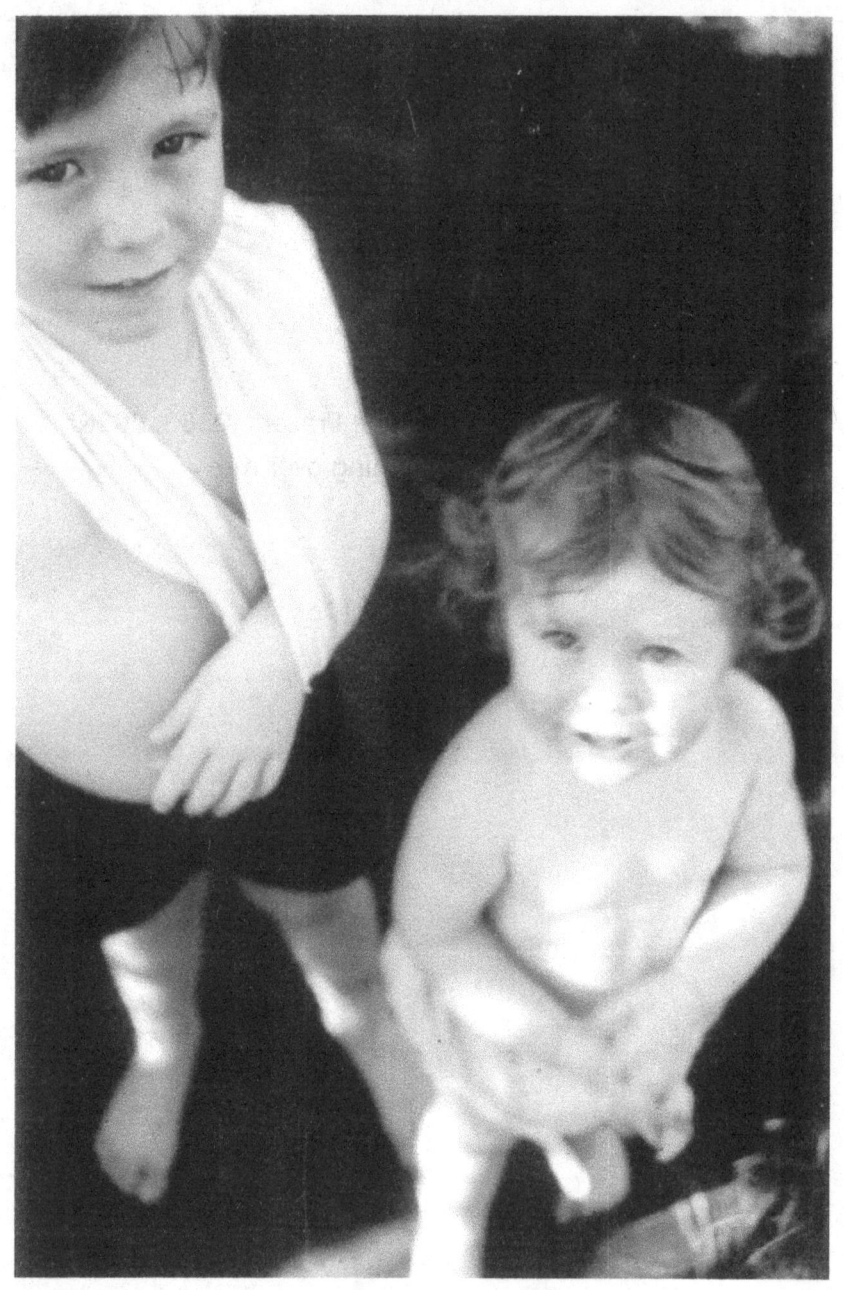

## About the Author

Bronwyn Frazer is a communications professional, writer, author, and holistic clinical nutritionist.

She has always been fascinated with the way people think, and why they do what they do. At the age of ten she started reading relationship and advice columns to get insights into people's problems and create her own answers.

With wisdom beyond her age, she has always been interested in the cycles of life and death and the tapestry that connects us all. Growing up in a large family, she has vague memories of road trips in a station wagon with no windows (as an adult she discovered her dad had bought and remodelled an old hearse).

Bronwyn has learnt to embrace change as part of her continuous growth. Her life has taught her that the road less travelled, while challenging, brings many blessings.

Having experienced many of life's big moments of change, Bronwyn has challenged herself to reflect and reframe so that she shifts the feelings of victimhood to build emotional intelligence and resilience. Through her work, she tries to keep the messages simple to help people look at situations from a different angle.

As an avid seeker of culture, philosophy, and history, Bronwyn has studied many ancient civilisations and travelled around the world and Australia. She now lives on Dharug,

Gundungurra and Wiradjuri lands in the beautiful Blue Mountains just outside of Sydney, Australia.

Bronwyn has a Bachelor of Communications with a minor in psychology and a Bachelor of Health Science in Nutritional and Dietetic Medicine, and a special interest in social dimensions of health.

# Introduction

*'The privilege of a lifetime is to become who you truly are.' - Carl Jung*

## Introduction

The inspiration and guidance included in this book came to me in an unusual way.

At the time, I was living in the lower north shore of Sydney without a car.

Mostly, I could walk or catch public transport. But towards the end of 2017, as my fur child started getting sick and frail, I realised that I needed my own transport.

So on weekends, I rented a car from a company a few suburbs away. Every Sunday after dropping the car back, I would walk the 5kms home. I've always loved walking – it grounds me – so I didn't mind.

One Sunday afternoon as I was walking home, I started getting a flood of ideas suddenly released from my subconscious posed as 'what if...' questions and answers. The thoughts came through my mind so fast, I had to quickly grab a pen and paper (I think the car receipt that first day) to capture them. This continued the whole walk home, with me stopping and starting to scribble notes.

Over the next few weeks, the same thing happened. My notepad kept filling up as I received more ideas, and different ways to look at the challenges life sometimes presents us with.

I wasn't sure if my notes were just for me, or to be shared with others in a book. So as life continued to get busy with work, and my decision to study another degree, I put the notes aside.

In 2019, when my dad started having more serious health issues, my life was in overdrive with work, studying, and juggling family and friendships. I was majorly stressed and didn't have the mental capacity to revisit my notes or write a book.

# Introduction

My dad was getting sicker, and intuition told me he didn't have much longer.

So in October 2020, when I decided to leave Sydney and move back to country New South Wales, my notes and belongings went into storage. Unbeknownst to me at the time, I would move many times including interstate and it would be four years before I could connect with my belongings again.

When I moved into my Blue Mountains home in May 2024, I unpacked my 'what if…' notes. It was shortly after this that I kept intuitively hearing and sensing, 'what if you don't have long to live… what needs doing?' Although I didn't feel I was dying – I knew it was my soul trying to get my attention.

There was an urgency to the message. But I ignored it, until I heard a similar message from one of my favourite teachers, Lee Harris, in July 2024. Then while talking to a beautiful local florist (Steph) about the book, she said 'it's not about you – it's for *them*!'

I will be forever grateful to both Lee and Steph for passing on these messages. It's due to them that I finally listened to my inner coach and finished this book in September 2024.

## My story

*'Life happens for you, not to you.'* – Abraham Hicks

I don't believe we should compare our challenges because all of us have different beliefs, paths, upbringings, and experiences that test us. Also, what is hard for one person is not necessarily for another.

But because you are reading this book, I want you to get

## Introduction

an insight into some of my biggest challenges to date. So, I'm going to share a little about me.

I was born into a family with five children (which would later expand into eight), to two incredible parents who somehow remained sane while raising us. Thankfully my parents had a can-do attitude and were extremely resilient. Throughout their marriage, they made hard decisions and many sacrifices to ensure we had the best health and education they could afford.

Looking back, my parents were perfect role models for me: they were brave, resilient, and challenged themselves in more ways than one.

My dad initially trained as a watch maker and mum as a registered nurse. Prior to my birth, they bought a jewellery shop in Kyogle New South Wales, a small town close to the border of Queensland. To run the business, they moved from Melbourne in Victoria, where they were born and bred, with five kids under seven. Mum nursed my brother Geoff (the baby) along the way as they travelled the 1,600 kms slowly in their small 1950's Austin Lancer. It took them several days to get to Kyogle. Moving required leaving behind their family, friends, and support networks.

In Kyogle, mum worked as a nurse at the local hospital between raising the family and having my younger brother and I. Dad ran the six day a week jewellery business, occasionally drove tourist buses on the weekends, and was very active in local charities. Mum and dad would continue to juggle family life while working and establishing more businesses down the track. To say they were busy is an understatement.

Growing up in a big family was fun, but it came with its own lessons. For example, I quickly learnt that life does not revolve around me (which is good training for when you

## Introduction

become an adult). I learnt to share, be considerate of others, and I learnt how to pick myself up when I fell over. I also came to understand that if I didn't do something myself, it may not get done. When you're from a big family you develop resilience, independence, tenacity, and the importance of teamwork.

My childhood was mostly idyllic until just before my tenth birthday. Unbeknownst to me, my parents were unable to afford the school fees. At the time, they had seven school aged kids, one of whom required specialised education for dyslexia. To support the family, dad looked around for other business opportunities.

A family friend and Bank Manager who had recently moved from Kyogle to the Hunter Valley, told mum and dad about a profitable business for sale. After investigating it, my parents bought an Italian restaurant (even though we weren't Italian and had no background in hospitality) off an Italian family in Muswellbrook, New South Wales. My dad used to joke that there were similarities between our restaurant and the one in *Fawlty Towers* (a popular 1980's TV show).

The people selling asked for a quick handover and thankfully this included training in traditional Italian cooking and running the restaurant. My sister Jo relocated first by herself and received 1:1 training. Within a few weeks of buying the business, mum and dad packed up our home and relocated six kids and a cat. Then for an intensive two-week period, dad was taught how to make the pizzas and mum the sauces and meals. This was the start of my love affair with authentic Italian food.

With the move and new business, each of us was challenged. We moved a few weeks before my tenth birthday, so I didn't get to celebrate with my friends. I found it hard

## Introduction

settling into a new school. I missed my best friend, but as time moved on, I made new connections.

However the next year when a new girl came to our school, I found myself in a group of three. I quickly learnt the meaning of 'two is company and three is a crowd'. Unfortunately, the new girl didn't like me. So she talked my so called best and sole friend into ganging up on me – two or more against one is never comfortable. I remember being called all sorts of names, sworn at (which was unfamiliar, because no one in my family swore), and being isolated and excluded. This was the first time I had experienced such intense and personal bullying. It made me feel sick and I didn't want to go to school. No one in the family knew what was happening.

One day at school, I told my classroom teacher that I felt sick and (as was the norm at the time) I was sent to sick bay. Then when no one was looking, I left the school grounds. After wandering around town for what seemed like a few hours, I ended up in a park, thinking through my options. This was the first time I thought about self-harm. I was ten years old. Thankfully my dad found me and took me home. In the next week, the girls at school were forced to apologise in front of my classroom teacher. They claimed they were 'only joking', but the hurt was long lasting. I became a loner hanging out in the school library so that I didn't have to talk to anyone. I felt safest there and developed a lifelong love for books and knowledge, especially history and ancient cultures.

After finishing high school, I lived overseas for a year as a Rotary exchange student. It was an eye-opening experience and forced me to grow up quickly. Dealing with constant change, moving every three months, meeting lots of new people, travelling, and giving presentations about Australia to

## Introduction

strangers helped me develop people skills. I will forever be grateful to both my parents and Rotary for giving me this opportunity.

My year abroad also gave me a taste for travel and adventure. I've since travelled extensively overseas and lived in America and England. I have also lived in all states of Australia, bar Tasmania and South Australia, and both Darwin and Canberra.

Moving within cities, states, territories, and countries brings unique challenges and stress. Every time you move you are forced to change and start again. You need to find a home, build new friendships, and connect with the community. I've often relocated without a job but thankfully after periods of unemployment (some longer than others), I've found my feet. I've changed jobs and industries more times than I'd care to write on my resume, but each situation has helped me develop new skills and meet amazing people, some of whom have become lifelong friends.

Romantic relationships haven't always been easy for me. But when things haven't felt right, I've been resilient enough to make tough decisions. This has included cancelling a wedding three months before the event. It was a massive, gut wrenching and heart-breaking decision because I had been with my partner for many years. When I made the decision to leave him, I also left our home, my friends, and my job, to relocate from interstate back to New South Wales. Looking back, I admire the brave person who made those decisions – it would have been easier to just get married, but I knew it wasn't the right thing to do. I feel that sometimes we need to be isolated (physically and emotionally) to find our truth and face reality.

While the ending of any relationship is challenging, the

## Introduction

death of loved ones has been even more confronting and painful. In 2009, one of my older brothers (Geoff) died in his sleep in Sydney. He was young, fit, and healthy. The autopsy was inconclusive so there was no physical explanation to help us understand the 'why'. But I've come to learn that some things in life just don't make sense.

Each family member experienced his death differently. My parents were grief stricken – no one expects their children to die before them.

For me, the waves of shock and grief alternated with sadness that I would never see him again or talk to him. I also had regrets. I hadn't seen him for more than 12 months because it was expensive to travel from Western Australia (where I was living) back to the east coast.

Geoff's death was preparation for my beautiful dad who died of chronic heart failure in 2020 – the first year of the COVID pandemic. Saying goodbye to a loved one during that time was particularly hard. Social distancing and health laws in New South Wales required that only one person at a time was allowed to visit him in hospital. Then when he died there were interstate travel restrictions and limits on how many people could attend his funeral. This meant that family from Victoria couldn't come to say goodbye. These restrictions added additional grief to an already tough situation.

As you grow up, you come to understand that life can at times feel like a rollercoaster – there will be ups and downs. But these days when challenged, I've learnt to adjust my attitude so that I move into acceptance faster.

At the time of finishing this book, I've fractured a bone in my right ankle. It was a bush walking accident. I'm getting about in a moonboot which is frustrating for someone as active and independent as me. But it could have been worse –

## Introduction

at least I didn't require surgery or a foot caste (which would have meant I'd be house bound). I'm reframing this as a 'temporary' situation. I know that this too is serving me because it is helping me to stay home and focus on finishing this book. Hopefully with rest, patience, and the right care, my ankle will rebuild stronger. In some ways, my ankle is a reminder of how to look after ourselves when faced with a tough situation or experience.

There is way more to my story, but it would take me a long time to talk you through it. Hopefully by sharing these few experiences I've given you an insight into my background and why I felt inspired to write this book.

Life can at times feel tough. Change and challenges are not always easy or pleasant, but they are a part of life. However, by reframing situations you can help yourself look at things differently and potentially clear heavy emotions faster. If I had read a book like this when I was younger, it may have saved me years of grief and professional counselling.

Introduction

# What if...?

I realise that the title of this book is a bit different. The phrase, 'what if...?' is often linked to negative outcomes. I used to think that way, until I started receiving inspiration for this book.

Through 'what if' questions, I was being encouraged to see situations and challenges from a positive or different angle. By doing this, I learnt how to shift my energy from feeling dis-empowered into strength and resilience.

Life has continuously taught me that I can't always control what happens, but I can control how I perceive things. Then, with self-awareness and conscious intention, I can choose to respond differently.

This book is a combination of the divine inspiration I got when walking home those afternoons, plus other life experiences. Each challenge has given me the opportunity to learn and grow.

All the guidance shared is to help you build self-awareness, so that you can grow from your experiences.

To make it easier for you to absorb, the book has been divided into themes.

You can choose to read *What if...* from cover to cover, or randomly choose sections to read. There is no right or wrong way; just what feels right for you.

I suggest that as you read through *What if...*, you write notes about your own experiences and what comes up for you.

Remember to be gentle with yourself as you read through this book. It has been created to remind you of your strength, not make you feel bad about yourself or others.

But, if any of the writing triggers feelings of guilt, regret,

## Introduction

sadness, or intense anger, please seek professional support to move through it.

As you read this book, I hope you remember that you are stronger, braver, and more powerful than what you currently believe.

Introduction

## Wisdom within

*What if...* was created to help you reconnect with your inner teacher and the wisdom within you.

There is an inner voice and an energy that some people connect with through religious or spiritual belief, and others find through self development. How you come to hear your inner voice doesn't matter, so long as you learn to trust it.

Learning to listen and allow love (instead of fear) to guide you is powerful. It reminds you that things don't happen *to you*, but rather *for you*.

When you embrace this mindset, powerful shifts in your life will occur, and as you change, the people and community around you will too. This is how we change the world into a place where people and planet come before profit.

Introduction

# Adopt a growth mindset

*What if...* was written to help you reframe your challenges and problems into opportunities for personal growth, learning, and strength.

By looking at challenges differently, you'll develop self-awareness and learn techniques to help you do things differently (if you choose to) in the future.

Personal growth is not easy, especially when you recognise that your words, actions, and energy may have potentially contributed to an argument, conflict, misunderstanding or problem.

However if you don't learn and grow from uncomfortable situations, you'll continue to attract similar people and scenarios to test you.

Don't beat yourself up when something makes you feel uncomfortable. It's more than okay. Just remember – everything that challenges us is an opportunity.

Be curious about your life, both past and present. Try to keep an open mind and heart to the suggestions presented in this book.

Use the 'Notes to self' section at the end of each short chapter to reflect on the situation and how you might relate. What did you learn? How did you grow?

These can be profoundly challenging questions. Though this book aims to empower you to move through the world with confidence, I strongly suggest seeking professional counselling support if these questions contribute to feelings of destabilisation or distress.

# 1

## Learning through relationships

*'Everyone is my teacher.*
   *Some I seek. Some I subconsciously attract.*
   *Often, I learn simply by observing others.*
   *Some may be completely unaware that I'm learning from them, yet I bow deeply in gratitude.'*
   *– Eric Allen*

## What if: you knew every relationship (even the difficult ones) offered a gift?

We are all teachers, because we influence everyone we encounter, even strangers.

We are forever pupils because life is continuing to teach us things.

Some of my most powerful teachers have been strangers. Coming into my life for a moment, they've provided me with sound guidance when I've needed it the most.

> 'Life's not about me; it's about we.' – Tony Robbins

Some relationships are more difficult than others. But these can offer powerful self-growth, learning, and insights for you.

Sometimes they teach you how *not* to show up in the world. Perhaps they provide you with an opportunity to speak up for yourself. Or maybe the experience is about learning how to set healthy boundaries.

At times challenging relationships may show you traits in yourself that you are not willing to acknowledge or accept.

In psychology, this is called 'mirroring'. Mirroring is not a bad thing. Once you acknowledge it, you can choose to come to terms with the parts of yourself you don't love, and change the behaviour that might be holding you back.

**Inspired thought:**
Every challenging relationship offers blessings in disguise if you are willing and open to reframing the discomfort.

What if...?

**Notes to self:**

When in a challenging relationship, ask yourself 'what gift or lesson is this person offering me?'

What did you learn about yourself?

# What if: you understood that hurt people hurt others?

Have you heard the saying 'hurt people hurt people'? It refers to people with unresolved wounds or trauma who project their pain (often disguised as anger) onto others.

For example – the child who was bullied at school, may grow up to bully people in their workplace.

> *'If you never heal from what hurt you,*
>   *you'll bleed on people who didn't cut you.'* –
> Yehunda Berg

While you should never accept bad behaviour, try to be compassionate with each person you meet, because all of us have wounds.

Try to develop awareness of your own wounds and triggers. This will help you learn from the past, so that you are less likely to transfer your hurt onto others.

**Inspired action:**
When interacting with triggering people, try to remain calm and clearheaded so that you don't respond with anger or transfer your frustration onto others.

What if...?

**Notes to self:**

What did this chapter bring up for you?

Is there a situation you need to let go of? If yes, what is it?

What old wounds are holding you back?

## What if: you could heal a relationship by apologising?

Do you struggle to say, 'I'm sorry'? Or do you say 'I'm sorry' for everything?

Depending on your childhood, you might have struggled with apologising – instead blaming others for your mistakes and accidents. Adults who haven't grown up carry this trait into their relationships and their workplace.

In comparison, some people say 'I'm sorry' for everything. This can be a sign of very low self-esteem; the person is really asking for acceptance and approval.

Knowing when to accept responsibility for words or actions that have intentionally or otherwise hurt others is powerful and involves emotional intelligence.

So, when you recognise you are in the wrong, speak to the person involved as soon as possible in private.

Alternatively, try this process.

**Inspired action:**

If you can't talk to the person face to face or on the phone, find a quiet place on your own. Turn off your phone, sit down, and then breathe deeply up to ten times.

Then, imagine the person is sitting in front of you. Mentally or verbally ask for your Higher Self and theirs to step forward.

In your mind or out loud, talk to their soul. Tell them that you are sorry and why. Breathe deeply and mentally listen for their response.

**Notes to self:**

What came up for you?

What did you learn about yourself?

How can you use this information to improve your relationships in the future?

## What if: you understood that no one owes you anything?

You may have inherited the belief that you should always expect something in return for things you do.

But what if you realised this is old, manipulative energy? What if you realised this way of thinking and being was unhealthy for both you and the other person?

Here's why.

When you constantly keep score of what you did for others and who (in your mind) owes you, you'll always feel like you're in deficit.

Plus, your relationships will be full of toxicity because you'll always be approaching people with a mindset of 'what can they give me'.

**Inspired thought:**

Practice giving without expectation, and you'll notice a positive shift in your relationships.

**Notes to self:**

Do you give with the underlying expectation that the receiver gives something back?

Where do you think this belief system comes from?

Are you willing to change?

## What if: you knew that your parents did the best they could?

> *'Love your parents and treat them with loving care.*
> *For you will only know their value when you see their empty chair.'*
> *– Anonymous*

You may feel hard done by your parents – what they did or didn't do for you as a child. But parenthood is tough.

There's no handbook to tell someone how to be a 'good parent' because there's no right way to parent or one size fits all. Why? Because every child is different, and every adult brings a different upbringing and values into the relationship.

> *'We will never know the love of a parent till we become parents ourselves.'* – Henry Ward Beecher

Our parents do the best they can with the knowledge they have of parenthood learnt through their culture, religion, beliefs, upbringing, and personal experiences.

Sadly, this might have meant carrying forward generational trauma from what their own parents did or said, or how society told them to 'be'.

However, some parents do make poor choices – even though they know better. This is harder to understand and reconcile. Seek professional support and advice if you need – you don't need to handle these issues alone.

**Inspired thought:**

If you don't clear painful experiences from childhood, you may carry this trauma into future relationships. Please be extra kind to yourself as you work through any issues this topic has raised.

What if...?

**Notes to self:**

Are you holding onto hurt from your childhood? Describe the situation here.

Can you look at this situation from a different angle? For example – what was going on for your parents at the time? What issues were they dealing with?

How could they have dealt with the situation better if they had access to some of the things we now know about generational trauma?

Think about your grandparents. How have their relationships potentially influenced your parents and their teaching style?

# What if: you said 'no'?

A lot of people have grown up being people-pleasers. In most cultures women have been expected to play this role.

For fear of hurting people, letting them down, or not being liked, I grew up being a 'people-pleaser'. I said yes to all requests for help and support, even though I often wanted to say no.

In my mind, it was more important to be thought of as a 'nice person' than it was to honour myself. This led to longer hours at work, attending social events that made me feel uncomfortable, and staying in unhealthy relationships longer.

With time, I have learnt to listen to my intuition. I now say 'no' to requests or invitations if I feel that I want to.

*'Stop trying to make everyone happy. You are not chocolate.' - Nick Ortner*

In life, there will be times when you need to place others ahead of yourself. For example – when raising children or supporting elderly parents.

But in other scenarios, listen to your intuition before saying 'YES'.

Why?

Because saying 'yes' when you'd prefer to say 'no' depletes your energy. This may trigger feelings of resentment, anger, and frustration – all of which are toxic for your relationships.

So before answering a request, listen to your intuition. Trust yourself and say no if that's how you feel.

What if...?

. . .

**Inspired thought:**

Nick Ortner author of *The Tapping Solution for Manifesting Your Greatest Self* suggests that when you are asked to do something, pause for a minute before responding. The pause allows you to breathe and assess if there's any hesitation in saying 'yes'. Then if you're still unsure, tell the person you'll need to get back to them. Set a timeframe for your decision so that you don't overthink it.

PS. If your answer is a 'no', don't feel the need to give an excuse. This is often where people-pleasers come unstuck.

**Notes to self:**

Are you a 'yes' person? If so, why?

How often do you say 'yes' when you really want to say no?

What healthy boundaries can you start to set up for yourself?

Who or what do you need to prioritise?

Who or what do you need to start stepping away from?

## What if: today you looked for the good in others?

*'When you look for the good in others, you discover the best in yourself.' – Martin Walsh*

While it is natural that you won't instantly bond with everyone, what if you let that person who annoys you off the hook? What if from today you looked for their positive traits?

By doing this, you might find you have different interactions with them.

You may find that your relationship improves to where it is easier to be with them.

Or you may find the universe intervenes, helping to reduce the frequency of you being together.

**Inspired thought:**
You're not ever going to get along with or be liked by everyone. The sooner you come to accept this, the less energy you'll waste.

Bronwyn Frazer

**Notes to self:**

Write down three positive things about the person who annoys you.

What are you learning from them?

What are you learning about YOU?

## What if: you realised that mean people help you grow?

*'No one can make you feel inferior without your consent.' - Eleanor Roosevelt*

When you are little, it is hard to believe that someone who is mean may be jealous or threatened by you.

When you're little, you also don't understand that sometimes they're being cruel to you because you're an 'easy' or 'safe' target for their attack.

As a child I didn't understand why some people were mean to me. Now that I'm an adult, I've come to realise that in every setting (be it school, home, or the workplace), there may be a growth opportunity in the discomfort.

Why?

Sometimes criticism or bullying can be a form of misdirection – so that people focus on you, instead of them.

Perhaps they wish they had the courage to be like you. Or perhaps they are afraid of being attacked because they are like you.

Although this doesn't excuse bad behaviour, life has continuously taught me that these people attack others to make themselves feel more powerful.

While bullying is never ok, and you don't need to accept it – there is always a growth opportunity in uncomfortable situations.

Most bullies get a kick out of people's reactions. On some level, it gives them more energy and confidence to keep attacking. So try not to react to their comments. You might find that by ignoring them or their behaviour, they stop bullying you.

But sometimes the bullies help us speak up for ourselves by calling out their bad behaviour. If you feel this is your truth, talk to the individual directly and in private. Calmly ask them why they are doing what they are doing.

If you don't feel you can do this, talk to someone you trust. Try to find peaceful and positive solutions to resolve the situation so that you can both move forward.

*'Situational variables can exert powerful influences over human behaviour, more so than we recognise or acknowledge.' – Phillip Zimbardo*

If a person is angry at you and it is out of character for them, there may be something else going on.

Perhaps someone got angry at them earlier in the day, and they couldn't or didn't stand up to that person. So, without meaning to, they have transferred their anger or frustration onto you.

Maybe they have a challenging personal issue they aren't handling well. Like a health issue or the death of a loved one.

Maybe they are using anger to cover their fears or insecurities.

Or perhaps as a child, they never learnt how to communicate effectively without getting angry or being critical.

Regardless of the reason, ultimately when someone is not

kind to you it's more about them – particularly if their response was unprovoked.

Of course, it is hard not to take it personally in the moment. In some cases, you may feel like you've come under attack.

If/when these scenarios occur – breathe, then ask the individual what is going on for them. Or alternatively you can walk away, then when you feel ready and (if you feel you need to) speak to the person at a different time.

Always calm down before responding so that you don't overreact and make a bad situation worse.

**Inspired thought:**
Sometimes there may be elements of truth in what seems to be criticism. Be careful not to perceive 'feedback' or 'room for improvement' as bullying.

**Notes to self:**

Describe a situation when you felt small. What happened? Who was involved?

What did you learn from this situation?

How could you handle the situation differently if it happened again?

## What if: you detached from the drama?

Drama can be addictive. Some people love watching, reading, or hearing about other people's dramas or challenges because it makes them feel better about their own life.

Others think life is boring if there is no challenge or conflict in their relationships. So, they go from one negative situation to another, often dragging friends or family into their problems.

How do you recognise a drama king or queen?

Easy! They thrive on exaggeration and often blame others instead of accepting how they've potentially contributed to the situation. If attention is not on them, they'll unconsciously create another drama.

Do you create unnecessary drama? For example – are you continually overspending (when you can't afford to), changing jobs within weeks of starting, or choosing destructive relationships?

Here's another example of how you may be creating drama. At one stage, a good friend of mine and I were mirroring each other in our relationships. We seemed to be competing to see who could go out with the weirdest guy! Although some of our stories were amusing at the time, in retrospect, we were both creating unnecessary drama in our lives.

All of us have a little bit of drama queen or king in us. But living this way constantly is stressful, tiring, and ultimately unhealthy for you and the people around you.

**Inspired thought:**
There will be times in life when things don't go right for you. But if you're continuing to attract similar challenging situations, perhaps it is time for self-reflection. Perhaps it is time to do something differently?

What if...?

**Notes to self:**

Where in your life are you creating unnecessary drama?

How could you start to shift your behaviour?

What drama are you willing to let go of? What do you need to do?

## What if: everyone looked for similarities, instead of differences?

*'Share our similarities, celebrate our differences.'*
– M. Scott Peck

Children are amazing teachers because they remind us to look for similarities instead of differences. I was reminded of this at my niece's birthday one year.

My niece 'Anna' (not her real name) asked if she could celebrate her fifth birthday with a party in the local park. Her parents said yes, and ten little people, plus their parents and some relatives, were invited.

Each relative was given a job. Mine was to put out party plates and monitor the food table in case the little guests needed help.

As I was doing this, I saw a beautiful interaction that touched my heart and made me smile.

One of my niece's guests, 'Sally' spotted a friend at another swing and invited her over. My niece didn't know the other girl, so Sally introduced them. The conversation went something like this:

'Anna, this is my friend from ballet. Anna, meet Anna. I hope we don't get you confused!'

To me, as an adult looking on, it would have been hard to confuse the two girls.

My niece is blonde and fair skinned, whereas the other little girl had black hair and olive skin tone.

What did this teach me? It reminded me that children see

connections – not differences. How amazing would the world be if we saw similarities instead of differences?

**Inspired thought:**
Children are our greatest teachers because through their innocence, they remind us to find connections and treat everyone equally.

Bronwyn Frazer

**Notes to self:**

Does this message resonate with you?

What did you learn about yourself?

## What if: you spoke up?

*'The standard we walk past is the standard we accept. What are you walking past?' - Anonymous*

When I was 16, a school friend and I experienced something I will never forget.

While we were eating our food at a café in Sydney, a homeless man walked in and asked the man behind the counter for food.

The café worker's response was volatile. He yelled at the homeless man as if he were a stray dog until he left.

My girlfriend and I looked at each other horrified. We both mentioned that we wished we had done something, but in the moment, we were embarrassed and shocked.

Future me would have done things differently. But it was an interesting moment in time, hopefully never to be repeated.

*'Nothing strengthens authority as much as silence.' - Leonardo da Vinci*

For change to occur, it takes one person to call out what is wrong. People don't change unless their words and behaviour are called into question.

So, if something doesn't feel right to you, please speak up.

It isn't always easy and sometimes you may be yelled at or told to mind your own business. But try – if not for you, for everyone who comes after you.

**Inspired thought:**

Throughout history there have been countless individuals who bravely spoke up for a cause, when it would have been easier not to. In doing so, they helped change the world.

What if...?

**Notes to self:**

When did you not speak up for someone or something? Describe the situation.

Why did you not say or do anything?

If you are ever in a similar situation again, what could you do differently?

## What if: you knew that nothing you have or own defines you?

*'There is nothing outside of yourself that can ever enable you to get better, stronger, richer, quicker, or smarter. Everything is within. Everything exists. Seek nothing outside yourself.'* – Miyamoto Musashi

Many people define themselves by their job title, their bank balance, what type of car they drive, where they live, and their physical appearance.

In doing so, they place a lot of emphasis and worth on external factors.

But life can change in a moment, forcing us to look at ourselves and life differently.

The COVID-19 pandemic did just that. Millions got sick, lost their jobs, income, homes, and personal freedom. Many people worldwide died.

While the pandemic was painful for all of us in different ways, it forced people to revaluate what was important to them in a crisis.

**Inspired thought:**
As you experience challenges, you may find that what you value changes. This is often a sign of personal growth.

What if...?

**Notes to self:**

Who or what do you value?

Are you placing too much value on what is outside of you?

Who would stand by you if you lost everything?

# What if: you took responsibility for your own happiness?

*'Happiness is a choice, not a result. Nothing will make you happy until you choose to be happy. No person will make you happy unless you decide to be happy. Your happiness will not come to you. It can only come from you.' - Anonymous*

Some people enter relationships with a conscious or unconscious mindset that 'this person will make me feel "happy" or "complete"'.

In doing so, they give their power away by relying on something or someone outside of themselves to help them feel happy, loved, and whole.

But in truth, only you are responsible for your happiness.

So, it is important to stop looking to others to 'fix' you or make you feel good about yourself.

Work instead on building a connection with you, so that you find how to make yourself happy.

**Inspired thought:**

Learn to make yourself happy by doing what you love, being authentic, and taking responsibility for YOU. Learn how to be comfortable with being alone.

. . .

## What if...?

When you do these things, your relationships will be healthier. But more importantly, your relationship with you will improve, because you'll connect with the divine love inside you.

**Notes to self:**

Are you trying to make someone else responsible for your happiness? If yes, who?

What makes you happy?

How can you incorporate more of this into your life?

What if...?

## What if: you understood that words hold power?

*'Words have energy and power with the ability to help, to heal, to hinder, to hurt, to harm, to humiliate, and to humble.' - Yehuda Berg*

Have you ever felt wounded by what someone said, even though they didn't use mean or abusive words?

Have you ever had a conversation where you felt that something wasn't right, but you couldn't put your finger on it? Has your intuition told you that you're being lied to, but you can't prove it?

Do you find yourself drained and tired, after interacting with some people?

If you answered YES, it might be because you've sensed from the tone, facial expressions, or subtext that they don't mean what they're saying.

Here's an example offered by *Ask and it is Given – Learning to Manifest Your Desires* by Esther and Jerry Hicks.

"'When a parent says, 'Don't you know I love you?!' in an angry tone the child feels anything but love because their intuition tells them otherwise.'"

*'Your word is your wand.' - Florence Scovel Shinn*

Every day is an opportunity to choose your words, and the thoughts that precede them, carefully. Words can build us up or knock us down. So, choose wisely. Use words that build you and the people around you.

**Inspired thought:**

When you feel good about yourself, you're less likely to criticise others.

What if...?

**Notes to self:**

Have you ever hurt someone with your words? When? What was going on?

How do you talk about yourself? Is there room for improvement?

## What if: you learnt to forgive?

What if forgiving someone could heal you? What if forgiving someone could help you move forward in your life? What if you knew that forgiveness is more powerful for you than 'them'?

In *You can heal your life*, author Louise Hay writes that when we refuse to forgive another, we only hurt ourselves. She believed that forgiveness is not about saying that what they did or said is okay. Rather it is about saying, 'I no longer allow you to hurt me.'

Forgiveness doesn't need to mean reconciling with someone who has hurt you. Nor does it mean relaxing important boundaries. You should never compromise self-worth. However, forgiveness may help you heal and move on.

> 'Forgiveness sets you free to move past the pain and on into a life of loving and serving.' - Wayne Dwyer

In the movie *My Greatest Teacher*, author Wayne Dwyer shares that his abusive father left when he was three years old. Then due to extreme poverty, Wayne's mother put the three children into an orphanage.

This situation triggered a lifetime of anger towards his father until one day, as an adult, he released it by yelling and screaming at his father's grave.

But as he walked away from the grave, he realised he had been angry for so long at someone he didn't know or even understand. He also realised that something must have happened to his father earlier in life that made him feel angry or rejected.

So, Wayne walked back to his father's plot and said, 'I forgive you'.

Wayne says he then felt instant relief wash over him, and the experience changed his life, relationships, and career. It was soon after this he wrote his first bestselling book.

**Inspired thought:**
Many of us carry pain from childhood. Unless you recognise how unhealthy this is, the hurts roll up into big snowballs that impact every part of your life.

Is today the day you set yourself free? Is today the day you forgive 'them'? Who or what can support you through this process?

Bronwyn Frazer

**Notes to self:**

What came up for you?

Who are you ready to forgive?

Are you willing to forgive yourself?

How will you use forgiveness to heal past and present difficult relationships?

## What if: you knew that self-love is crucial for your health?

*'The most powerful relationship you will ever have is the relationship with yourself.'* - Steve Maraboli

Although you may have been brought up thinking that loving yourself is vain, it's quite the opposite. When you are healthy and whole, your relationships will be too.

When you love yourself, you take good care of your mind and body. You say no to unhealthy relationships and respect your time and energy.

Love for self is the most important form of love because the way we treat ourselves shows others how to treat us.

Plus, it's good for your health. Self-love is crucial for lowering stress, positive mental health, creating healthy relationships and setting healthy boundaries.

**Inspired thought:**
Learning to like, love and accept yourself, just as you are, is a lifelong journey. But never give up!

Bronwyn Frazer

**Notes to self:**

When someone says, 'you need to love yourself more', how do you feel? What thoughts does that statement trigger?

Do you place others' needs before yourself? If yes, why?

Are you kind to you? If not, why?

What nice things can you do for yourself today?

What can you start to incorporate more of into your life?

## What if: you stopped letting the fear of rejection hold you back?

Our brains remember the risks associated with rejection. In ancient times, conforming to the tribe's rules and expectations was crucial for being fed, housed, clothed, and protected.

Conforming was crucial for survival. If you were different, you risked being rejected and cast out from your tribe. This potentially led to death.

*'The greatest trap in our life is not success, popularity, or power, but self-rejection.'* – Henri Nouwen

As children we grow up fearing rejection – first from our family, then friends, partners, and work colleagues.

Then the fear of rejection holds people back from being their authentic selves in relationships, work, and life in general.

But I believe it is better to be real and try, than live a life full of regrets.

**Inspired thought:**
If you avoid doing something for fear of rejection, you'll potentially stop yourself from receiving what you truly want.

Bronwyn Frazer

**Notes to self:**

What are you not doing, for fear of rejection?

Who or what is holding you back? Why?

Are your fears real? Or are they a story you keep telling yourself?

# 2
## Growing through discomfort

*'When we long for life without difficulties, remind us that oaks grow strong in contrary winds and diamonds are made under pressure.' – Peter Marshall*

## What if: you knew that resilience is a life skill?

*'Resilience is the capacity to withstand or recover quickly from difficulties.'* – The Australian mini-Oxford Dictionary (1986 edition)

Resilience isn't something that you inherit. It is a skill you develop when you make mistakes or when life doesn't follow the 'plan' you envisaged.

Some people develop resilience after the end of a romantic relationship. This is never easy, even if you're the one who has made the decision to call it quits.

When a relationship ends, you may experience the five stages of grief – denial, anger, bargaining, depression, and acceptance. But with time you come to understand that it's not the end of the world. As the saying goes – some relationships are for a reason or season and others are for a lifetime.

Most people develop resilience through experiences that test them. Here's an example from my life.

When I got offered a job in Perth, I was so excited. I'd thought about moving to Western Australia after finishing my first degree, but I'd never felt brave enough to relocate by myself. The job gave me an excuse to move.

As part of the adventure, my dad and I drove across the Nullarbor Plains together. It's a 4,000 km drive from Sydney to Perth and my car cassette player broke down within two hours of starting the trip. This gave us the opportunity to have deep and meaningful conversations along the way. It was a once in a lifetime opportunity that I still treasure.

Sadly, the job wasn't all it was cracked up to be. I had been told that I would have support staff. But when I started, I found out my one and only part time support person was about to go on maternity leave and wouldn't be replaced.

Then another situation completely out of my hands unfolded. The organisation underwent two state-wide restructures within six months. Half the people in my office were made redundant and lost their jobs. Unfortunately, the redundancies were staggered over three months. This prolonged the pain and discomfort for everyone. Some people who'd lost their jobs were crying in the office, some bragged about their payout figures, and others lost all interest in doing any work.

It was very depressing going to work. During the week we'd eat lots of muffins, then on Friday afternoons there'd be farewell drinks. I don't know how the State Manager came up with so many different farewell speeches.

Having recently moved, it was tough going through this alone. But within a few months, one of my brothers relocated to Perth. His support helped me immensely through a tough moment in time.

*'Out of your vulnerabilities will come your strength.' - Sigmund Freud*

We often develop resilience through uncomfortable situations, mistakes, accidents, and poor judgements. Although not pleasant, each of these can prepare us for our next big test.

**Inspired thought:**

Trust yourself. You WILL get through this, and when you come out the other side, you'll be stronger and wiser.

What if...?

**Notes to self:**

What big challenges have you faced so far in your life?

What did you learn from each? What new personal skills did you develop?

What have you learnt about yourself?

What can you congratulate yourself for?

## What if: you could feel better by changing your response?

*'You have complete control over how you feel at any time, good or bad.'* – Abraham Hicks

Life is not about what happens to you, it's about how you respond. In theory this sounds good, but it can be harder to put into practice.

Here's an example. One Christmas, my brother put a large plastic spider into my meal. At the time, I had my back turned and was talking to someone. When I turned back around to start eating, I saw the spider and started screaming.

After realising the spider wasn't real, I stopped screaming. Then I proceeded to angrily accuse my young nephews of putting it there because I'd seen them playing with it prior to sitting down to eat. When they denied putting the spider onto my meal, I got even angrier. I thought they were lying.

My sister took her kids into a separate room and asked if they'd put the spider into my meal. They said they hadn't but failed to mention (or chose not to mention) that my brother had put it there.

My reaction and anger didn't make sense to some family members. My dad defended me, explaining to everyone that I was tired after travelling and that I'm scared of spiders. But despite dad trying to smooth things over, to me the rest of the evening felt awkward. I felt 'bad' because without meaning to, I thought I had ruined (what had been) a nice family get together. The situation still makes me cringe today, but I can't turn back the clock.

It would be more than five years later before my brother admitted that he had put the spider onto my plate. He knew I have a spider phobia, so it was a mean joke. He said he didn't confess at the time because he didn't want to get in trouble. Unfortunately, it was too late to apologise to my nephews and sister.

Thankfully since then I've become better at recognising when I am highly triggered by something or someone. Then with conscious effort, I've been able to make a judgement call about speaking up or walking away.

I've gotten better at knowing when to give blunt feedback, and when to be more tactful. Instead of reacting with anger, I've also gotten better at taking a deep breath and counting to ten.

But I'm not perfect – it doesn't always work, and sometimes I don't like my reaction or response. However, like you, I'm a work in progress. So, I try to learn from every uncomfortable moment in time. I also try to be kinder to myself when things don't necessarily go well.

**Practice neutral detachment**

Do you easily get upset, angry, or triggered by others? If you answered YES, know that you're not alone. Me too. But by practicing neutral detachment, you don't need to feel or respond that way.

To explain what I mean, I'll give you an example.

Sometimes I need to work with people whom I don't like or agree with. When I feel this way, I often dread the thought of having to spend time with them in meetings. In my mind

I've already convinced myself that it is going to be a hard or uncomfortable meeting. Added to this, I've already told myself stories like this person is 'bad' or 'annoying' etc. In some cases, my thoughts have triggered anxiety.

To help me better manage uncomfortable situations and difficult relationships, a wise friend of mine encouraged me to neutralise my energy in advance. She suggested that I consciously let go of anger, fear, judgement, and negative expectations, *before* attending the meeting.

For me, this was powerful. I quickly learnt that by preparing my energy in advance, I was able to remain calm no matter what was said or done. Further by staying emotionally neutral, I was more in the moment. As a result, I'd often get a better outcome from the meeting.

By neutralising my energy I'm able to speak my truth in a grounded, powerful, calm, and tactful way. This makes me feel better, regardless of what's going on around me.

I encourage you to give it a go - see and feel what happens.

What if...?

**Notes to self:**

Think about a situation when you overreacted. How did you feel afterwards?

Who and what triggers you? Why?

What could you do differently when you see this person or have this experience again?

## What if: you trusted that your challenge has a purpose?

*'Out of difficulties come miracles.' – Jean de La Bruyere*

Life may seem tough at this moment in time. But when you look back, you will hopefully see the purpose and blessings behind your challenges.

As **The Astonishing Power of Emotions – Let Your Feelings Be Your Guide** author Abraham Hicks writes, sometimes a challenge helps us identify contrast or what we don't want. In doing so, we identify what we want and then focus on attracting it.

Or if your life is out of alignment with your soul, perhaps the challenge has arisen to inspire you to make important life changes.

Sometimes a challenge will help you develop new skills like independence, resilience, or the importance of listening to your intuition (instead of always trusting what others say).

In some cases, your challenge maybe an important part of the tapestry of many lives.

Here's an example. In 2009, when one of my brothers died in his sleep, I was heartbroken. He was young, healthy, and fit, so his sudden death was a massive shock.

But a good friend had lost a loved one in tragic circumstances only a few months prior, so she was able to relate to my grief and help me through mine.

Four years later, I was able to offer support to a good

friend when her brother died in his sleep. The cycle of compassion continued.

**Inspired thought:**
Please be gentle with yourself when you hit one of life's many road bumps. Ask for help and support to get through 'this moment'.

Once you feel whole again and if you feel comfortable doing so, ask your soul or Highest Self to share the wisdom behind the situation.

**Notes to self:**

Think about a big challenge. How did it help you learn and grow?

How can you help others, knowing what you know now?

## What if: you let go?

Are you trying too hard to control certain parts of your life? Are you trying to force things to happen? Are you an impatient person?

Did you know that when you push, control, or try to force outcomes in your favour – you are acting out of fear-based energies? Did you know that when you behave this way, you're not trusting in the universe's plan?

This way of being may get you results, but perhaps not the best outcome – especially in relationships.

> 'The minute we stop trying to control everything, is the minute God can finally lead us down the right path.' – Ashley Hetherington

I learnt this lesson many years ago when I had a hefty credit card bill.

At the time I had a good income, but after paying my living expenses, I was barely able to pay off the card interest each month.

I didn't know how I was going to clear the debt. So, I prayed to God for a solution, and it came in a way I never anticipated.

My tax return that year was substantial because I had submitted two years of returns, and my employer had taken too much tax out of my salary.

When my accountant told me what my return would be, I couldn't stop laughing!

With the money I was able to pay off both credit cards, buy a new car, and go on a holiday. It was such a wonderful feeling of freedom, and a reminder that everything has a way of working out.

**Inspired thought:**
Although we like to think we're in control, we're not. The divine always has a plan that is better than ours. So instead of pushing, could you let go? Could you trust that everything will line up in the right time, if it's meant to be?

What if...?

**Notes to self:**

Who or what are you currently trying to control? Describe the situation.

Why are you trying so hard?

Can you recognise the underlying emotions behind this situation? For example – fear of missing out, or if I don't do 'it' nothing will happen etc?

Could you let go of this situation? What thoughts does this idea trigger?

# What if: you trusted that everything will be ok?

*'Negativity can only feed on negativity.'*
  *– Elisabeth Kubler-Ross*

When you are feeling afraid or stressed, it is easy to imagine the worst things happening. But what if you realised you could influence the outcome through your thoughts and emotions?

Most people don't realise they can influence what shows up in life via how they think and feel. But science is now proving that your energy influences the outcome.

Here's an example that reminded me to trust I am protected.

When I was driving north from Sydney to Newcastle on the M1 Pacific Motorway one day, my car started to lose power.

I intuitively knew there was something wrong with the engine because despite my foot pressing the accelerator all the way to the floor, the car was rapidly slowing down.

At the time I was heading up Mt White. This is a dangerous part of the motorway, normally choked with three lanes of bumper-to-bumper trucks, semi-trailers, cars, and caravans travelling at 100 kms or more an hour.

Unfortunately for me, I was in the far-right lane of the motorway when my car started slowing down.

I knew it was an accident waiting to happen – the traffic was heavy, and trucks and cars were zooming past me. I had to act quickly.

There are no exit points on the right-hand side of the road.

So, this meant I had to get the car from the far-right lane to the far-left lane, then off the motorway.

Without panicking or envisaging the worst-case scenarios, I mentally asked my guardian angels for help.

Then in what felt like a slow-motion movie, I indicated left and weaved my way between the traffic coming up beside and behind my car. By this stage, I had no power or speed, so the car was using whatever residual energy was left in the engine.

Somehow, I managed to safely get the car across the traffic and off the motorway.

Turning the engine off, I viewed the traffic situation in my rear vision mirror. There was a continuous flow of trucks and cars speeding past my now stationary car.

My little car was shaking from the weight and speed of the vehicles zooming past. I knew I had to get out of it as quickly as possible.

Thankfully my dad (who was a champion driver) had given me loads of car safety talks in years prior.

He'd told me that if I ever had a breakdown, the best option was to get out via the passenger side and then move as far away from the car as possible. That way if my car got hit by oncoming traffic, I wouldn't be killed or injured in the collision.

After following his instructions, I called a tow truck. When the driver arrived, he was super negative.

In New South Wales, insurance companies only cover the first 50kms of towing for free. So even though I had comprehensive insurance, the truck driver said that because I was more than 50kms from the closest suburb or town, I should expect to pay up to $1,000 to get the car towed.

Then he explained he was only legally authorised to get

me off the motorway and to a safe spot. I would need to call my insurer and organise another tow truck to come collect me. So despite me trying to negotiate otherwise, he towed my car and I to a caravan rest point a few kilometres off the motorway, then left.

By this stage, I was quite distressed. It was a hot summer day, and I didn't have food or water.

As the ordeal of what 'almost happened' started to sink in, I felt like I was going to cry.

Seeing the tow truck leave me, a concerned beautiful, retired couple from Orange New South Wales came to my rescue.

The lady walked over to where I was parked and invited me to have lunch with them in their caravan. I gladly accepted the offer. It was the best egg and lettuce sandwich and cup of tea I've ever had.

After I thanked her numerous times, she explained that they had a daughter roughly my age. She said she hoped that if her daughter was ever in trouble, someone would help her too. I then started to cry. Angels are everywhere.

Every problem has a solution.

But even I didn't know how I'd get myself out of this scenario. I didn't have any friends or family to call because no one lived close to where I was stuck.

Back at my car, I looked at my number plates – they were Western Australia (WA) plates. I then remembered that because I'd only recently relocated from Western Australia to New South Wales, I hadn't yet transferred my insurance from Western Australia to New South Wales.

So, my car was still covered under the WA roadside insurance. This meant I was entitled to up to 100 kms of free towing. Hallelujah!

## What if...?

I called the insurance team, and they organised a tow truck to take my car and I back to Sydney. It worked out to be roughly 80kms, so the tow was covered for free by my insurer.

If you're open to them, miracles happen all the time. That day, I received several.

> *'There is a basic law that like attracts like. Negative thinking attracts negative results. Conversely, if a person habitually thinks optimistically and hopefully, his positive thinking sets in motion creative forces – and success instead of eluding him flows towards him.'*
> *– Norman Vincent Peale*

Do you expect bad things to happen, more than good things? If this describes you – please trust me. It's never too late to change your mind.

Some people may think of you as being naïve if you try to be positive all the time.

But I've come to learn that positive people often attract better outcomes.

I've also come to realise that angels (in disguise as humans) arrive when I most need their help.

**Inspired action:**
Most of us don't realise how negative we are. So here is a suggestion.

• • •

To test how often you're being negative, put a 'complaint jar' on the kitchen bench, your table, or desk. Each time someone (including you) complains or says something negative, get them to put an agreed penalty payment into the jar.

What if...?

**Notes to self:**

Describe a situation when you have expected a negative outcome but been pleasantly surprised. What happened and who helped?

What did this situation or experience teach you?

What do you need to be more positive about NOW? Describe the scenario.

Thinking about the situation, write three potential positive outcomes. Start each sentence with *What if...* then state what could happen.

Bronwyn Frazer

# What if: you learnt from your regrets?

*'I'd rather regret the things I've done than the things I haven't done.' – Lucille Ball*

I used to walk to and from school. On my way home, I'd chat to a beautiful older married couple who had lived in the same house for fifty odd years. The husband had a great sense of humour and I remember he used to love teasing me.

One day as I was walking past their house, I noticed that the lady was alone in her front garden. I asked where her husband was. Sadly, she told me he was in hospital. Although I couldn't drive at the time, I told her that I would try to visit him. Days went by and I didn't get there. Unfortunately, he died in hospital.

When I think back to the situation, I regret not making the effort to see him. Hospitals are sad and lonely places, especially for the elderly.

But as a 14-year-old I was distracted by other things. Plus, my parents were extremely busy people – they didn't always have time to drive me around.

*'I made decisions that I regret, and took them as learning experiences...I'm human, not perfect, like anybody else.' – Queen Latifah*

## What if...?

Regret can be a powerful teacher if reframed. Everyone has things they wish they'd done differently. However, with self-awareness, regrets can help you develop emotional intelligence.

Unfortunately, if regrets are allowed to expand in your mind, they can grow into feelings of guilt and shame.

If you don't clear these heavy feelings, over time you may become ill or attract unwanted situations.

If you need help shaking off regrets, talking to a parent, close friend, or counsellor might help you put things into perspective.

**Inspired thought:**

You can't take back time. Nor can you undo what has been said or done. So try to learn from your experiences and (if you feel to) make different decisions in the future.

**Notes to self:**

What do you regret doing or not doing?

Why do you have regrets?

Do you need to let go of some old beliefs that no longer serve you? If yes, what are they? Write them here and identify where they came from.

What could you do differently if there was a 'next time'?

Do you need to apologise to someone? Or do you need to forgive yourself and move on?

## What if: you faced your fears and danced with them anyway?

Sometimes fear is your intuition telling you that you're not ready for change or that circumstances aren't quite right yet.

But more often, fear is *False Evidence Appearing Real*. If you let it, fear will block you from achieving your dreams.

> *'One of the greatest discoveries a man makes, one of his greatest surprises, is to find he can do what he was afraid he couldn't do.'* – Henry Ford

Do you let fear hold you back? Or do you move through it?

In the book *Feel the Fear and Do It Anyway*, author Susan Jeffers challenges us to ask ourselves, 'what's the worst thing that can happen if I do X?'

When you ask yourself this question and listen to the answers, you'll potentially identify old beliefs that no longer serve you.

Then the choice is yours. Are you ready to step forward and be brave? Or will you continue to wait and have unfulfilled dreams?

> *'In any given moment we have two options: to step forward into growth or step back into safety.'* – *Abraham Maslow*

If you're still not feeling brave, think about this. *What if*...you were a superhero? What would you do without fear?

Author Joseph Campbell says that superheroes remind us of our true potential.

He also believed they carry our hope for humanity – that good will eventually overcome evil.

Try channelling your favourite superhero's energy into something you've always wanted to do. You might be surprised by the outcome.

**Inspired thought:**

When afraid, ask yourself, 'what's the worst thing that can happen?' Then ask yourself whether these fears are valid. If they aren't, keep moving forward.

What if...?

**Notes to self:**

Where in your life have you been holding yourself back?

What dreams are you yet to fulfill?

What one small step could you take today, towards creating your dream?

## What if: you loved your body instead of criticising it?

*'There's nothing wrong with me or my shape or who I am; you're the one with the problem!' – Jennifer Lopez*

When you were a baby, you thought your body was the most amazing thing. You loved every part of it and how it worked.

But as you grew older, people around you (potentially family or friends) started to criticise your appearance or the appearance of others. This prompted you to compare your body to others and as you did, you realised you were different, or somehow lacking.

Then you looked to the media, advertising, movies, the internet, magazines, books, and social media for advice and found even more negative messages.

If you, like me, believed 'them', you've carried these negative beliefs about your body into adulthood. As a result, when you look in the mirror, you criticise it.

Does this sound familiar? If yes, keep reading.

Criticising your body damages your self-esteem, confidence, and mental health. As a result, you're more likely to believe and accept other people's negative comments, which in truth are just a reflection of their insecurities.

## What if...?

*'Don't take your health for granted.*
*Don't take your body for granted.*
*Do something today that communicates to your body that you desire to care for it.*
*Tomorrow is not promised.'*
*- Jada Pinkett Smith*

Treat your body with love, kindness, and respect – especially when you are sick, or if you have a chronic illness, or live with a disability. Most of all – please treat your body with unconditional love. You may feel that your body has failed you, but it still supports you. Every day it performs functions that keep you alive and with people you love.

**Inspired thought:**

Please listen to your body and its day-to-day needs. Give your body the rest it needs when you feel tired. Fuel your body with nourishing and healthy food. Tell your body you love and appreciate it, every day.

Bronwyn Frazer

**Notes to self:**

When you look in the mirror, what do you see? How do you feel?

How do you talk to yourself?

What do you love about your body?

Are you comfortable with your body as it changes? If not, why not?

What does your body allow you to do? What are you grateful for?

## What if: you understood that anger can be a good thing?

Everyone experiences anger from time to time. It is a natural emotion which needs to be felt, expressed, and cleared in a healthy and nonviolent way.

However, as children most of us are taught that anger is bad. Perhaps because it makes the adults around us feel uncomfortable and embarrassed. Or perhaps because society tells us that being angry is something 'bad people' who can't control their behaviour do.

*'Use your anger wisely. Let it help you find solutions of love and truth.' - Mahatma Gandhi*

A man who used his anger wisely was Mahatma Gandhi (1869-1948), the lawyer and anticolonial activist, born in South Africa.

Gandhi led the peaceful civil disobedience campaign in India against Britain, which eventually resulted in the country's independence.

His action was spurred by the anger he felt at the injustices he and his countryman experienced, purely because of the colour of their skin.

Although Gandhi is long gone, his teachings live on in books like *The Gift of Anger*, written by his grandson, Arun Gandhi.

In *The Gift of Anger*, Arun writes his grandfather

encouraged people to ask themselves, 'why am I angry?' instead of reacting with violence.

His grandfather believed that once you found the source of your anger, you could find the solutions.

To become more self-aware, Mahatma Gandhi encouraged his grandson to keep an anger journal. In doing so, Arun was able to understand his anger and use it intelligently.

PS. Keep in mind that being angry all the time is not healthy for you or the people around you. If this describes you, please seek professional advice from a doctor or health professional. There may be an underlying health or emotional issue you are not aware of.

**Inspired thought:**
Anger when managed can be channelled into positive causes. Need more inspiration? Listen to Martin Luther King Junior read the *I Have a Dream* speech which he gave in in Washington DC in 1963.

What if...?

**Notes to self:**

Ask yourself – why am I angry? Write down everything that comes up for you.

Is there something positive you can do with this anger? If so, what?

How can you clear this anger, without hitting or hurting someone? For example – could you go for a nature walk, write in your journal, take a bath, go for a swim?

## What if: you waited instead of rushing an important decision?

*'Impatience can cause wise people to do foolish things.'* – Janette Oke

Do you rush your decisions, or do you take your time?

If you're like most people - the speed of your answer will depend on the circumstances. Of course, there's a big difference between trying to decide what type of hot drink to have versus whether to accept a job offer.

I know there have been times when I've rushed a decision for fear of missing out or being perceived as indecisive. This often results in regret.

*'Patience is the road to wisdom.'* - Kao Kalia Yang

Rushing can lead to poor decisions and less than perfect outcomes. So, if you don't know exactly what to do, please don't rush. Hit pause instead.

Your indecision or uncertainty may be telling you that the timing isn't right yet or that you are not ready.

Maybe you don't have all the information you need to make an informed decision.

Or maybe you need to wait for others to step forward and do their thing before it's the right time for you to act.

What if...?

. . .

**Inspired thought:**

Don't rush important decisions. Instead, learn to listen to your heart for alignment with the perfect timing.

**Notes to self:**

Are you an impatient person? If yes, do you know why you act that way?

Can you remember a time when you rushed a decision and it backfired on you? What happened?

What did you learn?

If faced with a similar situation, what would you do differently?

## What if: you realised it is good to accept help?

Many people (including me) struggle to ask for and receive help, either because they feel ashamed that they need it, or believe it's a sign of weakness. Others don't feel they are worthy of receiving help.

But what if you knew that asking for and accepting help is important for your mental and emotional health? What if you knew that the giver receives benefits too?

*'A balance of giving and receiving is essential for keeping your energy, mood, and motivation at a consistently high level.' - Doreen Virtue*

People who constantly give can become drained over time if they're not willing to accept help themselves. This way of 'being' can lead to chronic fatigue, anger, and resentment. That's why it is very important to balance giving with receiving.

**Inspired thought:**
Asking for help is not a weakness. It is a gift to you and the other person because it helps you both balance your energy.

**Notes to self:**

What do you need help with?

Who can you ask for support?

Where are you blocking yourself from receiving?

When people offer to help, do you accept their offer? If not, why?

Do you need to shift some old beliefs to help you be open to receiving?

# 3

## Dealing with death

*'To live in hearts we leave behind is not to die.'*
*– Thomas Campbell*

## What if: you knew love never dies?

The death of someone or something you love is extremely confronting. So many heavy feelings are triggered.

But what if you realised that love is eternal; that love never dies? What if you knew that the soul of your loved one is a constant companion, if only in your heart and memories?

What if you were open to the idea that they send you signs and messages, long after their death?

When one of my brothers died, I thought the world had ended.

I couldn't sleep, wasn't interested in food, and was an emotional wreck for at least a year. For the first time in my life, I understood the literal meaning of a heartache because my chest hurt, and nothing made it go away.

With time, the grief lessened. But what brings me the most comfort is that I receive signs reminding me of him, particularly when I am worried or low.

*'My heart will always wear the paw prints left by you.' - Anonymous*

The death of a pet can be just as hard as a human death.

When my little terrier died at age 16, the grief was intense. He had been my unconditionally loving companion through some very tough moments and big changes in my life.

But after his death, particularly in the first year, he sent me lots of reminders that his energy was still with me. This

## What if...?

included chance meetings of little terriers who looked just like him and had the same name.

Over the years I've found that these messages or reminders from my loved ones in heaven have brought great joy, comfort, and at times solutions.

**Inspired thought:**

When you see something that reminds you of your loved one, know that their energy is still with you.

Bronwyn Frazer

**Notes to self:**

What reminds you of your loved one?


What special sign could you ask your loved one to send?

## What if: you remembered death is part of the cycle of life?

*This was an incredibly hard chapter to write because I know how painful and sad the death of a loved one can be. But I encourage you to keep an open mind and heart, as you read the following.*

In late 2022, my friend Anne called an ambulance because she was experiencing intense stomach pain. The ambulance came quickly. But on the way to the hospital (which was only 10 minutes' drive from her home), she had a heart attack and died.

Her sudden death was a shock to everyone. She was fit, healthy and full of life.

The autopsy revealed a gallbladder infection which had turned septic, triggering the heart attack. Prior to her death, Anne had been complaining of stomach bloating and some occasional discomfort, but it hadn't been fully investigated.

I found out about her passing via a phone call from a mutual friend whom I hadn't heard from in years. It was a very weird conversation – there is no easy way to share that type of news.

As we discussed who Anne had been for each of us, we had a bit of a laugh and a bit of a cry.

Anne was a former work colleague, so I only knew parts of her story. The next week at her funeral I learnt more about her childhood and life before we'd met. It reminded me that we each know only a fragment of someone's life until we attend their funeral.

With the passing of time, it has become easier to accept

that Anne is no longer here. I try to focus on the crazy adventures we had and memories she gifted me with. Although I still miss her, I remember conversations that made me laugh, and her ability to make any event fun.

> *'It's part of the privilege of being human that we have our moment when we have to say goodbye.'* – Patti Smith

When death comes close to you with the passing of a loved one or a serious health diagnosis, it may stir up grief, anger, regrets, and memories of other people who have died. It may also trigger depression.

But death is part of the cycle of life. Like every creature, we are born and at some stage we will die.

In the western world, we fear death. We focus on our loss and the sadness of not seeing the person who has died again. We may also experience anger towards the loved one for leaving us – if not cleared, this can lead to feelings of guilt or shame.

Learning from different cultures may help with your grieving. For example - in Buddhism, death is believed to be part of 'samsara' - the cycle of life. So when a loved one dies, the relatives and friends of the deceased are encouraged to celebrate the life that was.

I saw this firsthand when I attended a funeral at a Buddhist temple just outside of Perth in Western Australia.

Even though my friend and I didn't know the person who had died, we were encouraged to witness the event. It was a beautiful ceremony in nature with flowers and incense burning. People attending were encouraged to share their stories about the deceased.

I'm not going to lie - it was an emotional experience, and some people were crying. But at the same time, it was a beautiful to be part of. It opened my eyes to a different way of viewing death.

A few years later, I shared this experience with a close friend whose mother had been diagnosed with terminal cancer. The extended family had been advised by the doctor that their mum didn't have long to live.

While she was still alive, my friend discussed the Buddhism concept with her mum and the immediate family. Her mum liked the idea and gave permission for doing things differently at her funeral.

So after her death, they sent 'celebration of life' invitations to the family and friends. At the celebration, people were invited to share stories (if they felt comfortable) that were meaningful to them, especially the funny experiences. Afterwards my friend expressed how uplifting the day was, despite their grief.

*'To live in the hearts we leave behind is not to die'. - Thomas Campbell*

Regardless of your relationship with the deceased, death is hard. But it is part of the cycle of life. So, when someone or something you love dies, try to focus on the love, memories, and blessings they brought into your life. Try to celebrate their life. Thank them for being part of your journey.

**Inspired thought:**
The death experience is different for everyone. Grief takes time to release and there is no time limit. There are no right or wrongs – only what is going on for you. Kindness to self, rest and patience is crucial for your healing.

What if...?

**Notes to self:**

What beautiful gifts and memories did your loved one leave you with?

How did they inspire you?

What did they teach you?

How can you celebrate their life?

## What if: by sharing your challenge, you help people heal?

Years ago, I wrote a story called 'Missing Mum' for the Mother's Day edition of Family Circle magazine.

I knew the story would be painful to write. But I also knew it would help people whose mum had died.

So, I interviewed three females - two friends and my cousin Jane whose mum died when she was six years old. I asked each person about their relationship with their mum, what they remembered, and what they missed.

Although reluctant at first to participate, each of the women later told me they got something positive from the experience.

One said that friends of her mum had read the story and loved it. They thanked her for bringing back good memories. My other friend said by sharing her story and reading those of the other women, she'd decided not to sweat the small stuff with her kids.

For my cousin Jane, being involved brought some much-needed closure. She was so young when her mum, Helen, died of cancer.

One of the things Jane shared in her story was that she couldn't remember the colour of her mum's hair. Her dad and grandma only had black and white photos of Helen - colour photos were less common in the 1960's. This left Jane feeling sad because she didn't know if they shared a similar complexion.

But after the story was published, a beautiful solution unfolded. A magazine reader, who recognised the black and white photo of Helen, contacted the magazine, and asked if they could put her in touch with Jane. Apparently she and

## What if...?

Helen had been school friends. She had colour photos she wanted to give to Jane.

How incredible is that? I love when the dominos of life connect so called strangers in unusual and powerful ways.

The story helped me too. It reminded me not to take my mum for granted and to regularly tell her she is loved. It helped countless others across Australia too, including the editor who cried when she first read it. Her mum had died not long before I submitted the story for publication.

*'Try to be the rainbow in someone's cloud.' - Maya Angelou*

Life can feel extremely lonely when you go through a big life change or a situation that tests you. But once you're out the other side, there is great power and healing in sharing your story, if you feel guided to.

The most successful artists and creators are the ones who use their personal stories and challenges as inspiration to create.

In doing so, they help people who are going through similar situations feel less alone.

**Inspired thought:**

Your challenge and how you got through it might be the catalyst for helping someone see their situation from a different perspective. It may also become part of their healing process.

Bronwyn Frazer

**Notes to self:**

Do you have a story that needs to be shared?

If so, what is it?

How can you share it?

What if...?

# What if: you knew you didn't have long to live?

*'Life is too short, so live your life to the fullest...every second of your life just treasure it...' - William Shakespeare*

Slightly depressing *'what if...*', but please stick with me.

Many people take it for granted that they will live until they are old. But in my extended family, there have been several deaths that remind me not to take old age for granted.

Each of my parents lost a brother before the age of ten years – one to Leukemia, the other to a house fire. My cousin died alone in her kitchen one morning, while her two young children were at school.

And my own brother died in his sleep at a young age. There was no time to say goodbye.

*'Never take life for granted. Savour every sunrise because no one is promised tomorrow...or even the rest of today.' - Eleanor Brown*

A few years ago, one of my lifelong friends, Rach, was taken to hospital. She had a fever and headache that wouldn't go away.

Tests showed she had meningitis – an infection and inflammation around the brain and spinal cord. Without proper diagnosis, she would have died.

But then worse news was to follow. The hospital x-rays and scans showed she had three tumours – one in her brain, neck, and one on her spinal cord.

For most people, this means a death sentence. But thankfully not for my friend. Despite being paralysed from the waist down after an operation to remove the neck tumour, Rach is still alive. Now she and her husband live every day as though it's their last.

And despite the odds, Rach has lived five years already beyond medical expectations. She is by all records a miracle and I for one (amongst hundreds) are grateful for that miracle.

**Inspired thought:**

Life is precious. One day will be your very last. There are no certainties as to when, but it could be sooner rather than later. Make every day count as though it is your last because one day it will be. Most of all – enjoy today.

What if...?

**Notes to self:**

Who needs to hear that you love them?

Who do you need to spend more quality time with? How can you make time for them? What can you do today?

What projects do you need to finish?

What do you want your life legacy to be?

## What if: you knew that only love is real?

Thanks to the movies, fairy tales, and media, love is often mistaken as something linked only with romantic relationships.

But I've come to realise that it is so much more.

Love is the 'money can't buy' factor. Everything else can be destroyed, stolen, or lost in a moment.

Love comes in many forms. It can be the unconditional love of your pet, the love you receive from parents or grandparents, or a bond with close friends.

Love is eternal. It lasts in our hearts and minds long after a death or ending.

*'There is no greater power in the universe than the power of love.*

*The feeling of love is the highest frequency you can emit.*

*If you could wrap every thought in love, if you could love everything and everyone, your life would be transformed.' – Unknown*

For years when I meditated, 'only LOVE is real' was the message I received repeatedly. I took it for granted as just something my guardian angels wanted to reinforce.

Then in a Brisbane café one day, I started having a chat with a stranger. During our conversation he shared that when his mother was dying, she kept repeating one statement – 'only LOVE is real'.

What if...?

After that day I never took the words for granted.

'Only LOVE is real' is a universal message for us all. Imagine if we all focused on love, instead of acting out of anger or frustration (which is fear in disguise). Imagine what we could achieve.

**Inspired thought:**

LOVE is your Higher Self in action, your North Star, and your inner compass. So, when you have an important decision to make, ask yourself – 'what would LOVE do now'? Then listen carefully to the answers you receive.

**Notes to self:**

What did this chapter bring up for you?

What did you learn?

# 4

## Creating consciously

*'You're braver than you believe, and stronger than you seem, and smarter than you think.'*
 *– A.A. Mine, Winnie the Pooh*

## What if: your life inspired others?

One Christmas when I was little, Dad received a present from the Salvation Army (the Salvos). Inside the small card was a handwritten note thanking him for all the help he had provided to those in need, throughout the year.

I was surprised by the gift and message. Until that day, I hadn't realised Dad was involved with the Salvos.

I knew that he was a member of Rotary and supported other clubs like APEX and the Lions Club, but I never understood what they did. It just seemed like they had lots of BBQs, and on Tuesday nights when Dad disappeared to Rotary, my mum took the opportunity to cook all the meals he hated.

But from that Christmas onwards, I watched my dad and witnessed his random acts of kindness.

Although he never talked about his good deeds, every now and then someone would thank him, or I'd hear a story about what he'd done.

Throughout his life he helped many strangers and their families purely because he thought he should.

Over the years I saw how both my parents helped their community. Small things (to them) done quietly, without a fuss. But in doing what they did, they inspired me to be the person I am. To think globally but act locally.

My parents were great role models for the world I would like to live in. For that, I will be eternally grateful.

Whether you know it or not, you are a role model for someone. It may be a family member, your children, a neighbour, someone you work with, or a stranger.

Someone is always watching and listening. That is why it is

important to make conscious decisions about your words and actions.

*'Be the change you wish to see in the world'. - Mahatma Gandhi*

What if you could inspire positive change amongst your family, friends, and community just by being YOU? What if you're the leader you've been waiting for?

If you're reading this book, I believe this is part of your life purpose. Here's why.

When you follow your dreams, you act as a positive role model for others and give them the courage to do the same.

When you speak up for a cause and role model your beliefs – you act as a way-shower for others.

When you radiate kindness and happiness, your energy lifts others up.

When you live an authentic life, you change your community and the world.

**Inspired thought:**

The world needs you to be different, to be brave, and to shine brightly. It takes one brave person to be themselves, before others will follow. It takes one brave person to change the world. I hope you find inspiration to do just that after reading this book.

## Bronwyn Frazer

**Notes to self:**

Are you afraid of being different? If yes, why?

Who told you it's not ok to be different?

Are you willing to believe 'them' still?

Where can you start to show up more in your life? Where do you need to be brave?

Who inspires you to be a better person? Why?

When you die, what legacy do you want to leave?

## What if: your random act of kindness could help someone view life differently?

*'Kindness is the language which the deaf can hear and the blind can see.' - Mark Twain*

When I was walking my fur children one morning, I noticed a handwritten note left on a car windscreen.

Being curious and nosey (two gifts my beautiful mother gave me), I stopped to read what it said. I'm so glad I did.

It was a letter thanking a 'kind stranger' who had left an envelope with $50 in it on the car windscreen the night before.

In the letter, the car owner reassured his donor that he wasn't homeless. He had slept in the car because he'd been on night shift and didn't want to wake his partner.

Providing his mobile number, he asked the person to contact him so that he could give the money back. He said if they didn't call him, he'd give the money to 'someone who really needed it'.

Did they meet? I don't know.

But this situation reminded me that good people are everywhere. We don't always know them, but they see us and want to help.

**Inspired thought:**
Random acts of kindness remind 'strangers' that they are

seen. And when done for family or friends, a random act of kindness reminds them they are loved.

**Notes to self:**

What random act of kindness could you do today to help a stranger? Tip – it doesn't need to be big or involve money.

## What if: you focused on today, instead of the future?

*'There are people who have money and people who are rich.'* – Coco Chanel

In *The Power of Now: A Guide to Spiritual Enlightenment*, author Ekhart Tolle writes when you enjoy this moment and today, you open the universal door to more good things.

So, while there is nothing wrong with hoping and dreaming of becoming rich, learn to appreciate today first and foremost.

Recognise and celebrate your blessings today and you'll start to feel like a millionaire. When you do, you'll notice a shift in how you feel and what comes to you.

**Inspired thought:**
Everyday you wake up is an opportunity to spend time with the people you love, do what brings you joy, learn something new, and have another adventure. So enjoy today!

**Notes to self:**

What makes you feel rich every day?

What do you have that you could not live without?

What daily gratitude practices could you incorporate into your life?

## What if: today you chose to be positive?

*'Positive thinking will let you do everything better than negative thinking will.'* – Zig Ziglar

Do you expect positive outcomes? Or are you always looking for what's wrong in your life or the world?

Did you know that positive thinking is good for your mental, emotional, and physical health?

Switching from a constantly negative mindset towards positivity takes years of practice but gets easier the more you do it. To help you adjust your mindset, try to spend more time with people who see the glass as half full.

**Inspired action:**
Everything that is created begins in the mind. So today, your challenge is to catch negative thoughts before you react or respond to something or someone.

Breathe deeply, count to ten, and let the negative thought go.

**Notes to self:**

Are you a glass-half-empty person? Do you tend to see things from a negative perspective, or get stuck in black-and-white thinking?

If yes, where did these beliefs come from? Who taught you to think this way?

What parts of your life would you like to see improvements in?

How could you turn this situation into one of possibility or optimism? Start your sentence with 'what if...?' then describe potential positive outcomes.

## What if: you knew you could create your own luck?

*'Luck is a matter of preparation meeting opportunity.'* – Oprah Winfrey

It used to stun me that people would say I was 'lucky' to travel a lot. Initially I used to say 'yes I AM' until I acknowledged I had made different choices to the person commenting.

You see, as someone who loves travelling, I have prioritised saving money to travel – instead of buying shoes, clothing, or, for a long time, a car.

As a result, I have travelled around the world, lived on several continents, and seen a significant amount of my own country, Australia.

My point is this – what seems like good luck to some is perhaps just the result of making different choices.

**Inspired thought:**
You create your own luck by keeping your heart and mind open to positivity and possibilities.

**Note to self:**

Are you placing limits on yourself about what you think you can and can't do? Why?

What makes you feel lucky? List five things.

## What if: your natural gifts could help others?

*'True happiness involves the full use of one's power and talents.'* – John W. Gardner

Everyone has natural gifts and special talents. When you use them to help others, you create positive change in your community, and the world.

Never underestimate your natural gifts and your ability to help others, by sharing them.

*'If you follow your bliss, you put yourself on a kind of track that has been there all the while, waiting for you, and the life you ought to be living is the one you are living. Follow your bliss and don't be afraid, and doors will open where you didn't know they were going to be.'*
– Joseph Campbell

Your passion (or bliss) is something that you love doing, are good at and comes naturally to you.

People who are passionate about what they do are often inspired to create businesses and products that help others.

Follow your passion, not just because it makes you feel good, but because it inspires others to do the same.

*'Your talent is God's gift to you. What you do with it is your gift back to God.'* - Leo Buscaglia

What are you good at? Could you use your talents to help others?

Do you have an idea that keeps popping up? Something you'd love to do or create? Is it something that could change the life of others, in a positive way?

If you answered 'yes', then maybe this is your sign to investigate your ideas.

Even if there is something similar already on the market, without copying it, could you make it even better?

**Inspired thought:**

Things that are created with the intent to help others tend to be way more successful than those based purely on making money. So, when using your talents, create with your heart, as well as with your head.

What if...?

**Notes to self:**

What did you love doing as a child?

What are you good at?

What makes you feel happy when you do it?

Could you turn your passion into something that could help others?

What can you do today to get started?

Who in your network (family, friends, community) can help you?

## What if: your donation could help many?

Early in my communications career, I worked at the Sydney office of a global charity.

Part of my job was to research and create media stories to support our fundraising campaigns.

I remember having a 'what if' conversation with my boss.

Something along the lines of, 'What if every Australian over 18 years donated $2 to our cause? We'd raise $20 million dollars!'

I'm not sure how much money we raised that year. I don't think we made anywhere near $20 million.

But the inspired idea made me realise that if everyone collectively contributed just a little towards a cause, we could create BIG changes for the better.

> *'Great things are done by a series of small things brought together.'*
> *— Vincent Van Gogh*

Many people want to help others, but they get caught up thinking they need to do something BIG.

But throughout my lifetime I've come to realise that small things are often very powerful.

So, if you feel strongly about something, it's your clue to help.

What if...?

**Inspired thought:**

Look for ways to be of service to others. Give to people because you want to give, not because you expect something in return. Know that somehow that goodness will find its way back to you when you need it.

**Inspired action:**

There are endless ways to help. Here are some suggestions.

- Volunteer to help at a charity shop, one day a week or month.
- On a regular basis, walk dogs from the local refuge.
- Take an older person grocery shopping or out for lunch.
- Mow a neighbour's lawn or bring in their garbage bins.
- Cook extra meals and share them with older neighbours or relatives.
- Instead of buying a coffee today, could you give the money to a charity? Or buy a coffee for somebody who might not be able to afford one?
- Rescue an abandoned animal.

**Notes to self:**

After reading this chapter, what do you feel inspired to do?


What one thing can you do today to help someone else?

## What if: you knew sharing increases your abundance?

What if by sharing, you could alleviate someone's stress and remind them that a higher power is at work?

Many of us don't see the way our small deeds help others, but I can assure you they do.

Years ago, a friend of mine told me that once when she was struggling to buy groceries for her young family, she received divine intervention.

On a day when she was particularly worried, a friend home delivered numerous plates of food left over from a work function.

Her friend didn't know about my friend's financial challenges. She just thought that with several kids to feed, the food might be helpful. Which, of course, it was!

> *'The measure of your life will not be in what you accumulate, but in what you give away.'* - Wayne W. Dwyer

There is a saying that 'sharing is caring'. But I've come to learn that it is so much more.

On an energetic level, sharing sends a message to the universe that you trust you are abundant. You are saying, 'I have more than enough to look after myself.'

When you do this, the universe will send you more.

**Inspired action:**

If you feel inspired to do something for someone else, don't hesitate. You might be part of the divine plan to help someone who really needs help.

**Notes to self:**


Ask your intuition, 'who needs help today?' Listen for the answers, then take inspired action.

## What if: I told you that you could change a person's day, just by smiling?

> 'Be the reason someone smiles. Be the reason someone feels loved and believes in the goodness in people.' - Roy T. Bennett

You never know how a smile may change someone's day or life.

At its most basic level, a smile offers visual recognition and acknowledgement that a person exists. This is particularly important for older people who may feel forgotten by the world, or others who might not feel 'seen'.

There are other benefits too.

Smiling at people is good for you and the receiver because it offers a positive exchange of energy between you.

Plus, when you smile at someone, it is very hard for them not to smile back. As a result, they're more likely to smile at others, carrying the positive energy forward.

Your health also improves. Smiling releases dopamine and endorphins, which make you feel happier. In doing so, they improve your mental health and reduce anxiety.

**Inspired thought:**

Life is short. Smile often and in doing so, you'll share your positive energy.

. . .

**Inspired action:**
Try a social experiment. Smile at three strangers today and see what happens. Assess how you feel afterwards.

Did it feel good?

Did they smile back?

Did you feel happier afterwards?

## What if: you knew kindness is a superpower?

As a child you may have been brought up thinking that being kind means you are weak or a pushover.

But this is not the case. It's the opposite.

Kindness is a sign of emotional intelligence and strength – especially when directed at someone who annoys you.

You never know when someone is struggling or has had a bad day. But one act of kindness can change their outlook. Kindness can help turn someone's inner light back on.

*'Love and kindness are never wasted.*
*They always make a difference.*
*They bless the one who receives them, and they bless you, the giver.'*
– Barbara de Angelis

More kindness is what the world urgently needs now to help people, animals, and the planet survive and thrive.

By being a role model for kindness, you can influence your family, friends, and community in a positive way. In doing so, you can help heal the world.

*'A single act of kindness throws out roots in all directions, and the roots spring up and make new trees.'* – Amelia Earhart

We all have busy schedules. But it is important to remember that the world is a lonely place for many – especially the elderly, sick, and people who live alone.

So, make the time to visit or phone someone you care about. In doing so, you will remind them that they are special and not alone.

**Inspired thought:**

So that you have the time and energy to truly give to others without feeling drained, you need to be kind to yourself first and foremost. So rest when you feel tired, sleep in without feeling guilty, read that book you bought ages ago, and go on holidays often.

What if...?

**Notes to self:**

Do you know someone who is a bit challenged by their circumstances? Could you visit today or call them?

Is there an elderly relative, friend, or neighbour who lives alone? Could you make up an excuse to visit them?

Who needs more kindness in their life?

What small thing could you do today, to lighten and brighten someone's day?

How are you going to show yourself more kindness?

## What if: by being generous, you inspired a better world?

I grew up being told by society that 'nothing comes for free'. As a result, I was suspicious of people who offered to help me or give me something. I didn't trust people easily and wasn't generous.

Thankfully, my dad was different.

He was kind and generous and gave without expectation. He role modelled a different way of 'being' in a world that was very masculine, aggressive, and at times toxic.

Watching him helped to soften my energy and with time, I became better at giving and receiving.

> *'I alone cannot change the world, but I can cast a stone across the waters to create many ripples.'*
> *- Mother Teresa*

Being generous is not just about giving people things – it's also about sharing your time. Are you generous with your time?

For example – when you take the kids to the park, do you turn off your mobile phone so that you can play with them?

When you eat with others, do you turn off your devices so that you can have a real conversation?

What if…?

**Inspired thought:**

Generosity is contagious. If you are generous with someone, they are more likely to share the positive energy with others.


Imagine what our world would be like if being kind and generous was normal?


**Notes to self:**


What did this chapter bring up for you?


How can you be more generous with others?


How can you be generous with yourself?

## What if: you knew your life has a purpose?

I believe that everyone has an important life purpose, or soul contract. It's like a plan with options that you put in place before you are born.

Your purpose includes the people you meet, where you live, what you do for work, and the relationships you have.

It may include becoming a parent, a singer, world leader, author, business owner, inventor, change leader, or something else.

> *'If you can't figure out your purpose, figure out your passion. For your passion will lead you right into your purpose.'* – Bishop T.D. Jakes

The things that you feel attracted to and have a strong urge to do are keys to unlocking your life purpose.

Then it's up to you whether you follow your inner guidance or not – there are no right or wrongs, just choices.

What if...?

**Inspired thought:**

Every life has a purpose – including when and how we die. This is especially hard to reconcile when a child dies, or someone is violently killed.

But through great tragedy often comes great change. Perhaps part of the individual's life purpose was to help raise awareness about an important health issue or increase government support for victims of violence. Or part of your own life's purpose might be to carry their memory forward.

**Notes to self:**

What did this chapter bring up for you?

What do you feel the urge to do?

## What if: you could help the earth heal?

*'Nature is not a place to visit. It is our home.'*
  *– Gary Snyder*


Worldwide, there are more and more big environmental issues that can no longer be ignored. Here are some examples.

Harmful chemicals from factories, mining, and farms seep into underground water tables, then into the ocean. In doing so, they pollute the ocean, kill sea life, and create further environmental disasters.

Mass clearing of trees in poor countries has led to land degradation, soil destabilisation, and erosion. Then, after heavy rain and flooding, mudslides have killed and destroyed everything their path.

As global temperatures rise, the water temperature is increasing and melting ice sheets at a much faster rate than predicted. As a result, low-lying islands and shorelines of continents, including America, are sinking.

*'We are on Earth to take care of life. We are on Earth to take care of each other.' – Xiye Bastida*

What if...?

**Inspired thought:**

All these issues seem bigger than one person. But your power lies in what you buy, who you vote for, and daily small actions that reduce waste.

**Inspired action:**

- Next time you go food shopping, buy only what you need and will use.
- Where possible, buy recycled furniture and household items.
- Before buying something new, do your research to make sure it is produced in an earth-friendly way.
- Avoid buying heavily packaged fruit, vegetables, and take away food and drinks.
- Support politicians who protect the environment.

# Acknowledgments

Mum and Dad – thank you for your endless love and support. Somehow, you 'got me', even when I didn't. For my big family who have helped me grow, literally and figuratively – thank you. Big love especially to Geoff, who died way too young.

A massive thank you to my adopted family who (in no particular order) includes Caroline Leonard, Kylie Tunks, Sharon Loersch, Chris, Chris Winkworth, Jessie Blake, Raelene Sutton, Lois Keay-Smith, Gabrielle Martinovich, Leonie Brettell, Stephanie Neal, Rach Thorpe, Jo, Brian and Orla Casserley and the fur team, Sally Bryett, Emma Stephens-Bridges, Meg and Hugh Cranswick, Catherine Kermond, Narissa Hamilton, Sal McDowell, Sophie Lee, Sarah Gillies, Rosa and Bertrand Nitrant, and Steph and Meagan (the Warin Wildflower team). Thank you for your support, friendship, love, and the endless laughs. My life is brighter because of you.

A massive thank you to the Hembury Books team – especially Jess Mudditt and Jessica Friedmann. Your professional support, feedback, and encouragement along the way has been greatly appreciated. Thank you.

Gratitude to all the writers, philosophers, way showers and thought changers who came before me. People like Oprah Winfrey, Esther and Jerry Hicks, Ian White, Dolores Cannon, Wayne Dwyer, Lee Harris, Cheryl Richardson, Louise Hay, Florence Scovel Shinn, Jamie Kern Lima, Rebecca Campbell,

Lisa Messenger, and everyone I have quoted in this book. Your wisdom continues to inspire me. Thank you for showing up!

Finally, thank you to all my teachers on earth and in heaven. I AM because of you.

With love,
 Bronwyn

www.ingramcontent.com/pod-product-compliance
Lightning Source LLC
Chambersburg PA
CBHW011550070526
44585CB00023B/2529